DEER IN THE HAYSTACKS
by
Dixie Partridge

Ahsahta Press

Boise State University
Boise, Idaho

Some of these poems have appeared in **The Montana Review, Poetry Now, Quarterly West, Snapdragon,** and **Sunstone**. "Angles," "At Gram's Grave," "Night Vision," and "Carrying the Past" received William Stafford Awards or Honorable Mentions (1979-1982). Washington Poets Association reserves anthology rights to these poems.

Editor for Ahsahta Press: Dale K. Boyer

Copyright © 1984 by Dixie Partridge

ISBN 0-916272-23-0

Library of Congress Catalog Card Number:
83-73659

my thanks to June and Gayle

Contents

1. Early Signs

II. Carrying the Past

III. Recurring Dreams

IV. Personal Effects

Introduction

Dixie Partridge is young to poetry, but she has learned well, either directly or indirectly, from teachers like William Stafford. **Deer in the Haystacks**, her first book, draws from terrain, in both the physical and conceptual sense, that is familiar to her. Some of her poems, like "Entering Smoot, Wyoming" and "Three-Room School," are rooted in place, but her territory is less spatial than it is temporal. In most of what I think are the best among the thirty-six poems in this volume, she works out a personal conception of time, particularly the past.

The past challenges any writer. How can one come to grips with the past, with memory, without dissolving into nostalgia? How can one be personal about memories without becoming maudlin? Partridge's first poem, "Early Signs," provides a good test case. She recalls her great grandfather who visted annually during the winter. As he sits on the porch awaiting a ride to "the next house," that of his daughter, Clara, the sisters "play games with his deafness." Partridge does not press the pathetic note here of a silent old man shuttled from relative to relative. Instead, retaining the perspective of the child, she notes that his hair is not really gray, but half dark and half white. Oddly enough, this apparently trivial detail is the central image (or perhaps the "triggering image") of the poem. Aunt Clara drives up, and great grandfather "gathers his bag/into both arms like it was a baby." This is as close to pathos as the poem comes. The way to keep memory from becoming an undesirable burden of emotional baggage is understatement. This how the poem ends:

> After he's gone, I stretch out in the sun
> on the winter lawn, which is still cold
> but drier than I expect. Looking closely,
> I see evenly intermixed with the dead grass,
> thin blades of green.

The great grandfather's half-dark, half-white hair has set up this image, which brings the poem to its subtle statement about life "intermixed" with death.

Partridge's use of the present tense in "Early Signs" is another way she has of dealing with the past so that it maintains its vitality rather than becoming a museum piece. Of course a number of poems do exist in the past (and in the past tense), like "Entering Smoot, Wyoming" and "Skin Deep," and certainly one of the most effective of these is the title poem, "Deer in the Haystacks":

> Down from the frozen hills, grey life
> came straggling; white hunger

looking for a reason.

Such openings compel me to read on. The poem "takes off." Against her impulse to feed them, her father "nudged," so they toughen their fences and cover their haystacks. The poem moves well from the general to the specific, to the "hard winter of '58," in which the dogs chase away a "gaunt doe." Partridge's closure in this poem is as firm and powerful as her opening:

> From the house later
> I could see faint steam rising above her
> to an ice-blue sky.

In a number of poems, like "Waiting" and "Windfalls," Partridge fuses the past with the present, but nowhere more effectively, I think, than in "Wilderness." She recounts the disappearance of a child from a family camp in Oregon:

> Weeks pass. The flawless trees go on
> with their silent enterprise above and beneath
> the forest floor, keeping what the people seek
> but fear to know.

In the second section, Partridge shifts to her own memory, of being brought home after a movie one night during a blizzard.

> I huddled on a straight-back chair, arms
> around my knees, not wanting my feet to touch
> the strange snow.

She does not have to say that she has experienced in some way a foreboding of the child's cold death. Her last line is sufficient: "I wanted never to think about that cold again." But she has.

Not all of Dixie Partridge's poems deal with the cold of Wyoming or with death, but these subjects are rarely far away. Even in the apparently light-hearted "Mariposa," the lilies, colored and shaped like butterflies, remind her of Great-grandmother Hanna and Aunt Mary Jane, and of "dead children buried in snow until spring." Shall she tell her daughter of this, she asks, "Shall I say we survive"?

> I tell her nothing:
> nothing but my laughter
> at the whirl of her delight
> as we wear butterflies
> home in our hair.

Only in the concluding poem of the collection, "Alone in the House: Late Winter," does Partridge, dreaming of an "avalanche . . . from the old farmhouse roof," conjure an image of the thaw:

> not the slow drip of water on limestone,
> wearing; not the downpour
> of rain winding rivulets
> to lower ground. What
> I hear is warm, fluent,
> filling all the hollow places.

Most of these poems show a clear grasp of craft, which is especially welcome in a first book. Above all, Dixie Partridge exhibits control over her materials. She has a firm sense of what to say and what not to say, and she is developing a voice which, I believe, will be distinctively her own.

Ron McFarland
University of Idaho
October, 1983

I. Early Signs

Early Signs

My sister and I can tell winter is over.
Great-grandfather Porter collects
his things into a leather bag darkened
with age, puts on his hat.
He sits on the porch chair in the rusty
odor of his ancient black wool,
waiting for his ride to the next house—
daughter Clara, eighty miles west.

We play games with his deafness,
see how close we can creep
before he knows we're there and jumps,
wild eyes taking a moment to remember
why. I go first, crouching up behind him
like our cat stalking birds.
I straighten, staring at his hair,
smelling my brother's Wildroot Creme Oil.
I see it isn't really grey—
half the hairs are dark, half white.
His head twitches rhythmically
to the left, as though connected to the tick
of the watch in his vest pocket.

Aunt Clara drives in. He pulls himself up
to the porch railing, gathers his bag
into both arms like it was a baby.
I don't move.
After he's gone, I stretch out in the sun
on the winter lawn, which is still cold
but drier than I expect. Looking closely,
I see evenly intermixed with the dead grass,
thin blades of green.

Entering Smoot, Wyoming Pop. 239

for Dad

We'd come here maybe twice a year
To see old Bill Stumpp.
His house was the brown fake-brick at the bend
Where the gravel lane joined the highway.

I'd mostly sit on his steep cement steps
(Cold on my thighs) and listen to you laugh
With him about the hunting trips
Or the time you camped all over Montana
In his old International.

You'd finally say *let's go;*
I'd watch to see in how much of a hurry
You were, and I'd always say—
Can we go the bumpy road, can we?
You'd never answer and I'd never know
For sure till we backed out the drive
And you turned the wheel in the right direction.

You'd gun it to get a good run;
I'd make my insides take hold
While dust shot up behind us
Like a Yellowstone geyser.
Gravel clattered a million sharp hits
Underneath the car.

Over each rise, one weightless
Instant trilled through me until I was almost
Exhausted when we got to U.S. 89.
You'd have a half-grin on your face
As the smooth quiet of the highway
Settled between us.

Once you turned off again
At the old church-house lane
And we went over it twice.

The China Closet

for Gram

The room is rose-toned:
coleus plants, the burgundy floral
of the carpet. In a shallow corner,
windowed on both sides, the china closet
holds lace-filtered light
and one small photograph;
wine-red and crystal pieces
from Sweden—sugar bowl and creamer,
four goblets; single glazed roses
on porcelain cups; in a polished shelf,
a crystal swan, floating.

A young girl approaches,
with one finger strokes
burnished wood, does not touch the glass
patterned in filagree from the windows.
She stares at the oval
grandfather she never knew—
he looks younger than her father.

She cannot know how it will change:
the china closet and its pieces
behind blinded windows
of a town museum, the swan
in blue fluorescence;
years and subdivisions away
she will miss this private corner
of her own history—
ruby glass and crystal
filling with sifted light.

Skin Deep

Grandmother's skin, fine parchment
veined with blue, wrapped
line of bone, stretched over knots
at joints paler
than white onion hearts
from Mamma's garden.

She reached for my hand,
didn't open her eyes but said
my name. I worked my fingers
into the palm, long-closed
by arthritis, found the skin
eyelid soft, smooth as the inside
of an onion peel.

I stroked, lightly,
wondering if my fingertips
pressed out ridges
on the other side.

In the end, I imagined her ascending
back to God and Grandpa Lee,
so thin sunlight seeped
through her body, a fiery silhouette—
the instant like the orange blink
of my eyelids against the sun . . .
then gone.

Seizure

for Lee and Ida H.

to survive one kick   one
iron hoof again and again
seven years when at any moment
the dull edge could take you
continue your deep fall   her words
caving in after   calling
calling you back
the moment on the farmhouse roof
hammer thudding off
to the ground   your heavy
sliding toward the edge
pitching at haystacks under close sun
heat bearing the slump of darkness
waking to timothy dust in your nostrils
your hands clenched   her voice lifting

you changed habits and avoided heights
always took someone along for the ride
shadow for shadow
and on that day   walking out alone
into fields   changing canvas dams
in the shallow ditches   you heard her
calling you back   heard her before she came
to find you face down in water
slight enough for your child's wading
heard her begging your name
the blackness iron   too heavy for rising

Deer in the Haystacks

Down from the frozen hills, grey life
came straggling: white hunger
looking for a reason.

When I was younger, I wanted to feed them;
Dad nudged against my impulse:
they were trouble enough, jumping haystack fences,
leaving hide on barbed wire and sometimes blood
    dripping a bright trail on crusted snow.
As it was, with cattle to winter, hard-grown
alfalfa stacks would run out before the long Wyoming cold.

The heavy-snowfall years, we battled the hunger
in them, their fear of humans left back
with higher altitudes, back with the rifle-crack
of hunting season. Heads down,
they'd stand their ground against our antics;
the dog had little more success, barking them halfway
across fields, where weakness dropped them.

We toughened fences and boarded up stacks,
fingers brittle and cold like the nails,
breath frozen in our nostrils.

The hard winter of '58, they came
right into the barnyard. One morning
I found a gaunt doe sniffing the milkhouse platform,
    legs bloody from pawing crusty snow.
I shooed her away; hooves clattered on ice,
legs shot out like strawsticks. The dog ran at her,
barking. She didn't flinch.

From the house later
I could see faint steam rising above her
to an ice-blue sky.

At Gram's Grave

Time is a string hung out of sight,
    Burning at this end;
    I'm alive in the flame,
    But not in the ash
    Nor the string.
Once time was a box
    You left at death;
    Never a pulse from nothing to nothing,
    The clock's tick only.

I could live with no shape for time—
Like the universe, uncomprehended.
But I dream time round:
Chimes from Gram's clock through the dark,
Slow rings of sound
Circling my bed
From the room below.

Grown, I bought such a clock.
    I sleep with that same smooth stroke
    Floating me back:
    Smoke rings
Ellipsing a fuse.

II. Carrying the Past

"There are people who always belong wherever Earth brings them . . . the rest of us
too, by the end of our days, learn to lean forward
out of our lives to find that what passes has molded
everything we touch or see, outside or in."

—*William Stafford*

Night Vision

Always before I've gone back in summer,
the farm green:
buttercup ridges, alfalfa, cattle-paths to hill pasture.

Now driving on ice around horseshoe bend,
I think beyond the farm to remember winter:
small town strata, fluff turned
ice in layers, crusting
the earth through blizzards and forty below;
living down under what everybody thought
they knew of others,
the green of private lives refrigerated
into molds, congealing and mute.

At Bridger Summit, I ease over.
Tires crunch against the bank plowed high
over the railing; no cars pass.
Ahead through twilight, sky and snow
blend, milk-luster; pines
are frozen glassy blue.
I think of that electric chill,
nerve white, the instant of a scald,
before the heat.

Winter never gets completely dark here.

I feel the engine ignite.
It will be slippery
down into the valley.

Angles

Gram died with most of her joints frozen
At right angles. My childhood watched
Her form brittle until she couldn't walk;
After that her frame assumed unchosen

Angles of the wheelchair and cracked like deadwood.
When I see my father now, I feel
A bloodrush back: his spine congeals
From the hips a rigid angle forward.

As in some half-forgotten dream
I've lived a future; it persists
In hard lumps on my wrists,
A bamboo gait and a grip growing lame.

Here where I live the trees grow at a slant
To northeast with the wind; they calcify
In traction. Across from my early
Years, trees grow straight along the ditchbank,

Each shaped like an ostrich feather.
Enchanted child, I think they've volatile
Powers to create the wind as they will
By fanning still air.

Wilderness

A Sacramento family camps on vacation
in Oregon. Their five-year-old vanishes
one smoky evening while they cook trout.
They stay on at the same campsite
as searchers cover the September countryside for miles.
Weeks pass. The flawless trees go on
with their silent enterprise above and beneath
the forest floor, keeping what the people seek
but fear to know. Birds and small animals
communicate their cries through darkening
days. It's nearly winter.
The people do not want to go home.

I remember a late night long ago,
being brought home from a movie I'd slept through.
Our door had blown open during a light blizzard—
the farmhouse stood dark and gaping,
a shallow drift across its floor.
I huddled on a straight-back chair, arms
around my knees, not wanting my feet to touch
the strange snow. I watched my mother
sweep it through the doorway, wipe linoleum
and chair legs before she helped me
into cold pajamas and sheets that had frozen
on her line before being brought inside to dry.
I wanted never to think about that cold again.

Wind Chimes

I

Late autumn winds grow gusty.
Through my open window fall
notes the texture of water, silver-
coated yet clear.

Five a.m. Dark. One more hour sleep.

I curl into the slumber of childhood
on the farm, pre-dawn milk pails
clanging, sounds below-zero
carried through frosted windows,
air metallic as the sounds.

In my slow stir, my long turn
toward the other side of my bed
I see, dreamlike,
my mother's hands clustering pails,
her quick steps past the water trough
where she breaks ice; the long,
slanting pulls of milk
chiming into the pail,
foaming upward; steam
rising in the cold of the stall.

Five a.m. Dark. One more hour sleep.

II

Frozen figures of laundry
lurch forward, back
in the wind. Thin-man
underwear curtsy to levis,
towels bob, scrape sheets
starched with frost.

Unstrung, the puppets tilt
through the doorway, piled-
high in her arms. She props
them near the stove, the wood box.
Frost flying, the sheets crack,
make tents over chairs.

We watch angles and effigies
wilt, Dad's long johns
ample again, flopping wet.
No place to sit. Every space draped, ghostly.
Our breath humid in the scent of washday.

III

Ivory rings on the harnesses
chink like metal in the cold.
The sorrels steam, large muscles
working the field of snow,
hay piled-high on runners sledding homeward.

Dad has shed his jacket after pitching,
his breath gusts white
against the distant blue of January,
bushed brows and nostril hair
turn frosty.

I am bundled under hay and cold,
pulsing with clear rhythms of the harnesses,
only my face bared, my breath
catching as fine snow
rises in white mists around us.

While Pruning

What tree would shape itself like this?
Symmetrically stocky, branching out wide
a foot above the earth, its center opening
to sun. Harvesting will be within reach.

Perhaps we learn from the haphazard—lightning,
disease, hungry deer in winter—to cut cleanly,
paint to seal the wounds.
Gram used to say *leave them be*

when we wanted to prune the lilacs
crowding her yard path.
Each year arthritis calcified more knots
into her joints, decreed

her movements painful, brittle,
restricted to the house and to the porch
where she sat with her lilacs for sun.
They stretched around her, shielding

the skeletal eighty pounds, knees that would not
unbend, hands that would not open.
My aunts would offer
there'll be more blossoms

if we cut them back . . . but no one pruned
at all until after she died.
We have to duck those lilacs even now
to get to the porch when we visit my father.

He allows them whatever space
they reach out for.

Willows

to my younger sister

Pasture sod overgrows the rocky
creek bed, deadening
liquid echoes of our shouts—
the water dammed upstream,
funneled to sprinkler systems.
Willows around the farmhouse have matured,
softening the angular two stories.

When Dad tore out
the poplars we had climbed for years,
replaced them with willows from the creek,
I felt barren: the girl on the slope
of a certain painting, only the farmhouse
ruling her horizon.

I rehearsed my leaving, made myself
outgrow the absent trees,
listened to the creek garbling
destinations. I ignored
your half-hearted nests in willows
along the bank. We mouthed
hard silences into separate
fables for telling ourselves through winter.

In the desert where I live
I watch the river: willows
bear the first aura of green,
keep the color when others turn.
My sight holds them till they are lost to grey,
broomy structures and the flowing river
charcoaled still, the water's surface iron.

Waiting

for N.

Think back to Wyoming: great snows
hardening in layers
like an endless white scab.
The snow-ice holds for weeks
into spring, when the air
softens.

We know more about winter now, the need.
More alive in that cold storage,
fragile breath wafts
like a genie from a bottle, re-enters
unseen, trailing the slightest taste
of metal. The sky,
ice blue, keeps its distance.
Frozen and muffed, stands of pine
no longer listen.
The absence of that listening
leaves the quiet
no place to go, makes it build,
cubic and tactile.

Through the long cold, insulated
against sun, the earth collects
its own heat—until one day
you walk over shrinking crusts of snow, cave
downward; your feet
touch a steamy warmth,
waiting.

Sources

We have only just admitted
to one another our wounds,
tongues salty in their lick
as tears loosening the backs of our throats.
Out from grey memory,
the colors have started, thick
with self, like mud streams.

How you remember it—
the younger sister, the *other* one—
the fit of our childhood
still tight as the laced high shoes
we had to wear, rubbing
red, hand-me-down circles around our ankles.

I open enough
for touching; old encroachments,
the dual ownership of everything we shared
sagging to one side
like the springs of our upstairs bed
those twenty years ago.

We retrace the frosty origins
our breathing sketched
on winter glass above our bed,
knowing the source
of such flow
must be a warm spring
or a melting glacier.

Windfalls,
Poem For My Younger Sister

As children, we couldn't even
gather orchard windfalls
without quarrels and bitterness;
I didn't guess you tried to be
like me, that you never felt
equal.

Our easy talk last summer,
after years
of having children, living apart:
I see you in your child-body
crying in the backseat corner
of our green Dodge, Dad telling Aunt Leora
she doesn't do anything well.

And now, after eating windfall fruit
those years, having to save the best
for sale at roadside stands,
you write how good it feels
to bite into the season's ripeness,
the most perfect apple from your one
backyard tree: taste the crispness,
sweet juices running.

Carrying the Past

It's here in the decaying wood of the barn,
  in dust and sweat coated on leather in the harness room;
  along rocky remnants of ditchbeds, roughly
  filled after sprinkler pipes were voted in.
It lingers in layers wallpapered on high ceilings
  of the house Great-grandfather built; in the scent
  of lilac bushes grown twenty feet high, crowding,
  trellising the path around the back corner.
It sizzled in bread my Swedish grandmother fried
  after I brought her morning cream; lumped
  with sugar held on her tongue as she drank Postum,
  Mormon coffee, every morning.
It became part of the warp left in my dad, growing up fatherless
  to farm with his mother; the silence he set between us;
  the farm work my mother still does, what he expects.
It shows in the slant of his back, arthritic,
  as it showed in knots on Gram's knuckles
  and in rigid angles of her joints.
It was pulled on with the long stockings and garter harness
  I hated and had to wear till I was eight;
  carried in the water bucket and to the woodbox, always gaping.
It circled us through long Wyoming winters;
  grinned at our scrambling to move the galvanized tub
  further out of sight behind the stove
  if a caller dropped in on Saturday night.
It hid under rock we lugged from plowed furrows;
  mixed with dirt in my shoes, the strain of horses at loads.
It crept into my disbelief that things could get so bad
  they had to borrow my seven dollars, shoe-boxed
  away—one for each year, from Gram.
It's in the old Swedish phrases, misplaced and mispronounced,
  that pop from my lips in strange flashes to connect
  somewhere far back;
And in my caution as I shift these layers: down under—
  rawness . . . or satin of new skin?

After Harvest

for my mother

You take long walks through these stubble
fields and along back roads,
head scarved in printed cotton,
his old brown wool bulky around you.
You do not stop in open places,
but near sheds or in trees
along the creek. These days,
he grows even more silent,
as the farmhouse is silent, as though
he assumes a stance—the shape of a future
he wants you to acknowledge.
The last child, a daughter,
married, moved north in the spring.
Summer was bearable:
working the farm with him as always
you could stay exhausted, delay
feeling. You wonder if you will cover
the silence by talking to yourself, wonder
what to say. You notice where fence posts sag,
drab siding where paint has worn from sheds.
You establish a regular route, an acceptable
pattern for the present: out past the barn
to the willowed creekbed, over rocky slopes
past sheds to Swenson's lane. You stop here
where an old Dodge, windows intact,
is buried under an avalanche of leaves,
patches of sycamore trunks around you
exposed as if the bark can't stretch enough
to cover the painful swelling underneath.

III. Recurring Dreams

One Winter

That year I was glad for the snow
I hadn't missed since leaving mountains
for a wind and desert town.
Snow was more trouble than fun here.

But after that June labor lost
my heart-flutter of a child—
fetus they called it,
screamed it—Nothing
else on the earth withered.
All summer I hated the loud
flaunting greens.
At least the browns of autumn
were condoning.

Grateful that the desert shunned color
I drabbed through rains melding
with the muted leaves and lawn
draining to sludge.

Then
when a freak whiteness
pillowed everything, suddenly
the silenced world withdrew
enough
and I went out to hear
the white breath in my lungs.

Basement Houses

From ashes, your house rises
two cement feet above earth:
black-topped, the stairwell angling sharply
heavenward like an air shaft.
Your children inhabit underground
like prairie animals.

Remember your early visits to the farm?
I envied your two-story, you—our basement house.
You know me better now.
And I know the weight of your darkness—
eyes enlarging on what they can't find,
blue-black veiling panes, all transparencies
compressed opaque.

You learn to recognize certain feet
passing the window near the stairwell,
senses turned upward to air,
for glimpses just above eye-level.
Your children play on the black roof.
They hate washing low windows, dusty
and cobwebbed overnight, wish them
bigger and clearer at bedtime.
They listen for other sounds
than traffic, branches in wind.
Lights burning late, they crawl
into sleep, ears fine-tuned
to all possible footsteps on the roof.

Behind Drawn Shades

They sit, dispensing silences
like pain pills, each hoarding
against what waits and hardens
further in, crusted as clay pots
empty on the side-porch.

A low table spaced between them
holds prescription vials and two
insulated glasses: his and hers.
T.V. tranquilizes
against telephone, former church-friends,
a daughter checking in.
The clock's chime is turned off;
only if the television runs out
will you hear the tick.

The one plant in the dim room holds up
its final leaf: a mottled claw.
What was soil is parched in
from sides of the hand-made crock,
impervious to watering.

Sense from the Past

I

A strangeness in my mother's voice
dragged me from sleep.
She hurried, wrapping my month-old brother, limp
in blue patchwork. I was left
to telephone the doctor: tell him he's bled for hours . . .

Smallness in my voice wavered
but I got the message through,
went to her room, stood by the crib.
Dark-edged crimson soaked the sheet and mattress,
in my breath: a humid, almost sweetness.

I stood until nauseous, then sat at the edge
of her bed thinking of the smell,
recalling the slight form
against new bedding
his first night home.

I let nothing move forward in those hours,
not thought, not daylight.
I moved from there
into a farm life that forgot
once he came home again.

II

At certain times
colors have smell

grey—the mousy
scent of the granary

pale blue—icy clearness
like the sky at twenty below

and red—the damp
dread of time passing

when you must have it still

Recurring Dream:
Leaving the Valley Where I Grew Up

Always it begins at the farmhouse:
the drive through town—Main Street's
arch of deer antlers—down through the narrows
along Salt River.
Always the road changes
in the climb out of the valley:
mountains, soft with pine, become
great slab cliffs, the roadway
fills with rock.
I turn back, not knowing
how I missed U.S. 89,
why a simple journey
turns desperate.
Trying the side roads along the reservoir
I find again the familiar
water the color of jade, willowed
springs, the end of the shale road
or a loop that circles back to the highway
climbing into rockslides I cannot scale.

Sestina

He writes rains have brightened leaves;
colors from the mountains reverberate to the daughter
who is startled at the facets his words
can carve. Silence carved an exquisite pain,
ice-sculptures between them, when her father
worked the fields. Now when he writes she sees

in his italic handwriting what he sees
on the farm: the brilliance in dying leaves,
the sky withdrawing its deep blue. The father
never spoke such things to his daughter
when she was there to hear. Or perhaps the pain
soundproofed the spaces surrounding his words.

The letters, amazing her with words,
began years after she left. What the sky sees
is the river, a satin ribbon between them. No pain.
When the distance grows too great, he leaves
the farm, follows the river to his daughter,
three states away. What greets the father,

but hardly touches the father,
are her brief smiles holding cautious words,
house chores keeping the daughter
from the tactile silence she sees
blocked out in her living room. He leaves
after he has recognized the old pain.

In time it changes hue: the pain
clarifies, translucent. The father
looks at her, at the sky, at the leaves
through the pain. He writes his words
meticulously; in them he sees
dissolving pain flow toward his daughter.

The letters are rare and brief. The daughter
opens her own white offering of pain,
stares at her form curved into its hollow: she sees
spring snows melting, her plowing father,
the harvest after planting—his words

gathered into bright crimson like the leaves.

Autumn touches the daughter, lives in the father.
A softer pain distills from the words,
colors. She sees more than the leaves.

Hypothermia

He was sixty-nine like your father,
found cold in his bed, fetal—
the mattress a cover for loose cash.
You wonder about his family—
what might have meant revival.
There was the heater in his bedroom—unplugged,
no sign of illness, a little food in the house.
Eight inches of snow pillow
his porch and sidewalk, the sterile passage
broken by footprints from the postman
who finds old mail in the box.

    You write weekly to your father.
    He has come to hate Wyoming winters,
    lasts them out with four tons of coal,
    thermostat at eighty, electric
    blankets "the blessing of the century."

Authorities say there's no reason,
no reason. You try to fill in
what's left out of the story, fabricate
disease, a wife
dead he wanted to join.
It seems very easy: closing
of eyelids, fading of warm
impulses to and from a brain.

    You remember a fire banked just right—
    the open oven a hearth
    where you hoarded extra warmth against
    icicles at windows and three more months of winter.
    When he kicked at the back door
    she let him in with a flood of cold,
    new calf sprawling from gunnysacks in his arms.
    You sat high on the woodbox to watch
    revival on the oven door: the calf rigid
    on its side, icy wet and blood-streaked,
    a Holstein eye shocked solidly open.

    After rubdown with burlap, its hair

dried in peaks and swirls, the body relaxed
to a curve, legs drawn under.
You remember thinking how simple
it looked—life easing into it that way—
as the eyelid closed.

Three-Room School

Peeled gray, a box more narrow
than I remember; high panes closed
by dust and old weather;
grounds too hard and dry for weeds.
Across the back fence is Thorton's field
where we played Fox and Geese in winter,
away from Old Bagley's principled face,
the paper snow-flaked
windows on the other side only a front.

Pick-ups rattle past on old U.S. 89,
but out in Thorton's field, the new, limited-
access highway curves wide from the mountains,
cuts through twenty farms—my father's
among them—to by-pass the town's first
golf course. The small ghost of a dust devil
see-saws across the yard, falters
in the large "O" where jump ropes slapped—
tough, long ropes our fathers used
for tying steers: missing meant your legs
burned tell-tale red.

Once Valdee Swenson ran off with our rope;
later, a conspiracy of Levis
tied me on the ground to the back fence.
Harold Mills (fists for hands)
passed yeasty beer in brown vanilla bottles—
the impudent tongue of the school bell
clanged over the tarnished silence,
dust settled in my face.
Fourth grade—already counting my choices
in District 19, held down
with flattened pain in my throat.

Grandfather's Place

I sense the old farmhouse, solid
beneath vinyl roof and siding—a presence
holding others: Charles and Priscilla, three generations
who somehow keep the marrow of this place
from strangers who live here.

A slab of patio
where the cellar-house stood—
shading it: ghosts
of huge poplars, arranging their arms
for climbing. From branches,
you can see the hen-house
collapsing, a wagon tongue
growing into the ground, sprouting thistles.
Low places in pastures
keep the memory of grandfather's pond
gone thirty years.

The aged dirt lanes I walk
through alfalfa dead-end
at fences, concessions to the freeway.
The neighbor's field is subdividing,
split-levels rising in rows.

In a certain dream,
I am in the future. My children
shout from resurrected trees,
new lumber heals the loft of the barn,
wagon spokes turn, blur,
lichen-free. In the fields:
the second-coming of the ponds,
ducks native again to our voices.
And down from the soft pine,
deer turn their knowing eyes
to our innocence.

IV. Personal Effects

"This tree knocked down by lightning—
and a hollow the owls made open to rain.
Disasters are all right, if they teach
             men and women
to turn their hollow places up.

"The tree lies stretched out where it fell in the grass.
It is so mysterious, waters below, waters above,
so little of it we can ever know."

—Robert Bly

Visit

You have come down from valleys in mountains
with your grief. Time enough later
for paying heed to desert winds,
clouds of dust that gather on horizons.
For now, we walk out against the sky,
discover the desert for its small comforts:
greyed mauve and copper along the river
where broomy structures bare themselves
to the coming winter. On the opposite bank,
earth has caved into the slow current
uncovering streaks of raw umber in the ashen soil.

Here the river bends its steel surface
among more shades of gray
than autumn colors in your mountains.
Yet you say you feel at home here,
with nuances the broad spectrum of sky
spills far into evening.
Even a winter without snow gives camouflage.
We wound groundnests with our feet before we realize.
Around us, owl and bobwhite cry out
against our careful clumsiness,
their habitat an open secret.

Stay for a while, friend. Wild geese
stroke the neutral sky, their calls
a pointed prophecy: this,
no season for planting.

Quickening

My ribs remember . . . you thumped
against night. First-year cries invade it.
You attack day before first light, dishevel crib,
ransack the house at your level: raccoon ritual.
In the yard you finger fence-links,
learning edges.

Your walk is run and stumble;
carried, you push legs against me, pump
us like a hand car down some endless track.
Even your hugs are kinetic, hands
patting my shoulder blades,
knees pushing up, fetal.

Poking buttons until we play
your music—switched-on Bach or Mills piano—
you sit center-floor to wave the beat.
When brown eyes glaze with fought-off sleep
you let me cradle you, arms
flailing.

At last you quiet. I hold
the moment: body easing to mine, breath matching.
I deliver you to bed, smell dampness
at your hairline; you quiver
a slight moan, like a small animal,
dying.

Mariposa

A field of landed butterflies,
Miranda says, alighting near them
to cup small hands over each.
Her field is a slope
on rocky foothills, the winged-
flower a distant relative
I introduce: Miranda, worthy of wonder—
Mariposa, fairy lantern, sego lily,
butterfly. She samples the name,
chants *Mariposa, Mariposa,*
as she flutters among them.

Shall I tell her of the frailness
of butterflies, of this flower
as Grandmother told me—that few
children survive on the manifold
beauty of sego: mother and sister and hunger
crouching to dig morsels of root.
Shall I begin with Great-grandmother
Hanna or Aunt Mary Jane,
with root cellars and failed crops
or with dead children buried in snow until spring.
Shall I say we survive.

I tell her nothing:
nothing but my laughter
at the whirl of her delight
as we wear butterflies
home in our hair.

"Shades of the Prison-House"

"Where is it now, the glory and the dream?"
—Wordsworth

for Anne

Startled awake, I meet my wailing
child on the dark stairs. He screams
at my sudden, silent appearance.
His body is rigid, his pulse
pounding into mine. He cries *Mamma,*
Mamma, as though I have not come.
His eyes haunt me to an edge
I remember, a place more savage
for being in the mind.

Finally his body eases
against me. Our breathing
flickers in the darkness.

After the moment of his birth
I saw his eyes, aghast
at that edge, ready
for terror. I remember
wild eyes of my great-grandfather,
    almost deaf, when a sound
    jerked him from that sheltered place
    he had tunneled;
trapped eyes of my grandmother
    who at the end called us
    by strange names.

Hemorrhaging from miscarriage,
unable to move or speak as I awoke,
I tried to hurl the terror
from my own eyes
to those oblivious around me.
It is like a cry issued

toward God, toward an immortal
humanity in the universe,
a cry we live in desperately
as the thread of light
subsides.

Snowy Owl
at Woodland Park Zoo

Stoic, he eyes
the curious and the unimpressed alike—
a white prince,
origins of captivity scattered
like rubbish on pavements
circling, circling. . . .
Within smeared glass,
bearded claws commemorate
the casual nests, private young.

I tell myself I've humanized the owl,
born to this habitat
like I to twentieth-century man,
bloodlines stretched thin,
beyond origins of conscience—
what we are meant to be
winging, distant on the pale horizon;
what we are becoming
soundlessly approaching
unseen, to fall
accurate on its prey.

Personal Effects:
Closure of the Church at Osmond, Wyoming

I.

From a country school, I spent
recesses one autumn watching workmen—local farmers
like my father who paid their share in hours.
I played on the subflooring, my feet calling up
hallowed echoes from the crawl space,
kingdoms to come rising in daydreams to open rafters.

My father's silence somehow lifted here,
and I didn't miss a chance to believe
his affection, others out of the picture.
I pretended he was building just for me:
this gift of scented lumber,
nails gliding in under strokes almost tender.

I wished it could go on forever,
resisted the pasty smell of plaster but loved
the narrow strips of pine that finished the outside,
felt the loss of it under white paint.
The small steeple held the only colored glass—
green of broad leaves translucent against sun.

II.

Now, pale wood of dislocated pews
reflects the sunlight, padded seats
in damask rose. I wonder what will be done
with the mural—Christ assuring
awe-struck faces of fishermen, their fish
glistening, still heavy in the net.

On Writing About Childhood

What I have to say, I have not said.
                    —Robert Bly

When the snow came, it stayed
longer than the winter
our calendar from Grain and Feed
zoned with red: first day of autumn
first day of winter, first day of spring.

Walking out through drifts, your legs
worked hard climbing in and out
of each step, soon gave way to the ache
and followed sunken prints back
to wintering in at the farmhouse.

Sometimes, after the creek froze over,
for that short time before banks deepened,
you could walk easy over the hollow crush
of snow on ice, stretch yourself down past
frosted willows to the rim of last light
where the south pasture ended.

Returning is never the same: through luminous
nightfall you walk the landscape of a film negative,
silvery and unreal, yet exactly
familiar. The smooth lane of the creekbed
casts the shallow bootprints white,
white all the way back.

Links

for J.

Like a frost,
Dust covers the black shoes in your closet;
I don't wipe them clean.

I walk around sawhorses and two-by-fours
Day after day in the garage;
I know I should move them.

My mind saves images
For your return. My body waits
To sit beside you at the table, to feel warmth come
Home these early winter nights.

Like the farm wife who still wakes
Before dawn
When there are no longer the cows to milk,
The children to raise, nor the husband
To nudge from the bed,

I expect you.

Alone in the House: Late Winter

I

Near midnight, the house quiets,
insulated against snow.
I move soundless over carpet.
Downward: only the soft
trailing of my gown on the stairs.
Nightlight shadows slide
over the cold tile floor. Footfall
soundings vibrate to my skull.
I cover a child who at this moment
turns toward me, his breath
licking my arm. The bunk creaks.
Overhead, a clock begins its chime.
Two strides to each slow stroke
I stalk the stairway, glide
through dark toward lamplight
in my room. I lie in bed,
hear the pulse in my skull,
am prowling still, alien.

II

I wake to the pulsing,
walls returning the rhythm.
Alarmed by the avalanche
I have dreamed from the old farmhouse roof,
I grope for meanings—
shift from frosted windows of my childhood
to the gray windows above my bed, the utterance
of the house around me. I think
chinook . . . think *thaw.*
The sound of steady dripping
percolates through the house, my senses:
not the slow drip of water on limestone,
wearing; not the downpour
of rain winding rivulets
to lower ground. What
I hear is warm, fluent,
filling all the hollow places.

Dixie Henderson Partridge was born in 1943 at Afton, Wyoming, and grew up on a small farm near Afton which was first settled by her great-grandfather, Samuel Henderson, in the 1880's. She graduated with a degree in English from Brigham Young University in 1965, married a chemist, Jerry A. Partridge, and moved to Richland, Washington, where she is now part-time writer and full-time mother to six children. She has worked with several children's and youth groups and has taught a series of parent education classes, enjoys music, clothing design and construction, and discovering new books of poetry.

She began writing poetry in 1978 after suppressing the urge to do so for some time. She enrolled in a graduate class with Irish poet James McAuley through Eastern Washington University and became involved with Mid-Columbia Writers and northwest poetry workshops. Dixie Partridge's writing first appeared in northwest haiku anthologies; several of her poems have placed in the annual William Stafford Awards in recent years. **Deer in the Haystacks** *is her first book.*

Ahsahta Press

POETRY OF THE WEST

MODERN

*Norman Macleod, *Selected Poems*
Gwendolen Haste, *Selected Poems*
*Peggy Pond Church, *New & Selected Poems*
Haniel Long, *My Seasons*
H. L. Davis, *Selected Poems*
*Hildegarde Flanner, *The Hearkening Eye*
Genevieve Taggard, *To the Natural World*
Hazel Hall, *Selected Poems*
Women Poets of the West: *An Anthology*
*Thomas Hornsby Ferril, *Anvil of Roses*
*Judson Crews, *The Clock of Moss*

CONTEMPORARY

*Marnie Walsh, *A Taste of the Knife*
*Robert Krieger, *Headlands, Rising*
Richard Blessing, *Winter Constellations*
*Carolyne Wright, *Stealing the Children*
Charley John Greasybear, *Songs*
*Conger Beasley, Jr., *Over DeSoto's Bones*
*Susan Strayer Deal, *No Moving Parts*
*Gretel Ehrlich, *To Touch the Water*
*Leo Romero, *Agua Negra*
*David Baker, *Laws of the Land*
*Richard Speakes, *Hannah's Travel*
Dixie Partridge, *Deer in the Haystacks*
Philip St. Clair, *At the Tent of Heaven*

*Selections from these volumes, read by their authors, are now available on *The Ahsahta Cassette Sampler.*